Published 1974 by The Hamlyn Publishing Group Limited
London · New York · Sydney · Toronto
Astronaut House, Feltham, Middlesex, England
© Copyright 1974 The Hamlyn Publishing Group Limited
Printed in Spain by Mateu Cromo

ISBN 0 600 38686 4

This is the way we
Sow and Grow

by Jennifer Curry
illustrated by Robin Laurie

Hamlyn
LONDON · NEW YORK · SYDNEY · TORONTO

Gardening is a pastime which fascinates children of all ages. They love to grow things, for the development of a seed into a flower seems like a bit of magic and even a young child requires only a little supervision to help him enjoy the adventure of gardening. Nor is it necessary to have a big garden—or indeed a garden at all—to achieve bright, rewarding results. A few jars and saucers on a window ledge, two or three plant pots on a balcony, give immediate scope for a variety of activities.

Gardening out-of-doors, however, is always lots of fun, particularly if a few simple rules are followed. Make sure your child is suitably dressed—wearing sturdy shoes or boots, and if there is likely to be any danger from poisonous insects, he should wear gardening gloves too. Overalls, or a large pinafore, well-provided with pockets, could save clothes from irreparable staining or damage.

Children will need their own set of tools if they are going to enjoy their gardening to the full. The simplest gardening jobs will seem impossible if they have to struggle with a spade or fork that is almost as big as they are—and nothing will discourage them quicker. To begin with, a child will need a trowel, a spade, a fork and a watering can. For the gardening tasks that involve cutting, it would be better to let little hands use round-edged scissors instead of expensive secateurs that can be difficult to manipulate.

For many children the first steps in gardening are helping parents and there are many jobs that even the youngest can do. Clearing up fallen leaves, cutting off dead heads, watering, raking and light digging, carting away weeds in a barrow—all will accustom him to simple routine gardening tasks and more importantly, he will enjoy himself as he learns!

Many other activities that children enjoy so much—painting, drawing pictures, decorating containers, making little animals from the seeds or flower petals they grow or collect—can be linked to gardening, and will often help to occupy the long gaps that inevitably occur while things are growing. There are lots of bright ideas in this book for decorating pots to hold growing flowers, turning walnut shells into boats, fir cones into ducklings and poppies into endearing little dollies, to name only a few.

Since children are nearly always very impatient, and easily get bored if there is nothing to see for their hard work, it is a good idea to let them begin several of the projects in this book at the same time. Then slow growing activities can be combined with quicker ones, and the handicraft suggestions can be made in between times. For example, while they wait for some seeds to germinate out of doors, they can be watching the progress of the peas growing in jam jars *and* making the doll's house to go with their garden-in-a-seed tray. In this way the waiting periods will be much less difficult and their interest more likely to be sustained.

It is important to make sure, of course that all materials used are completely safe. Only non-toxic paints, and preferably non-inflammable glues should be available to children.

All of the seeds and plants mentioned in the following pages grow perfectly well in most kinds of ordinary garden soil, but the new soil-less composts are much lighter and cleaner to use, especially for indoor gardening. They also give excellent results. If children find difficulty in sowing small varieties of seeds, like lettuce, try using the pelleted ones, which are easier to handle.

The activities outlined in this book should keep children happily occupied throughout the year. But more than this, it could lay the foundation for a hobby which will give them life-long pleasure, as well as making them more aware of the natural world around them.

Plants are Alive

Plants are like you. They need to eat and drink if they are to grow, and sunshine if they are to be healthy, in the same way as you do

YOU WILL NEED:
warm water
sugar lumps
a small glass or jar
a spoon
an onion, with roots and leaves showing

1 Plants cannot eat solid food. They cannot crunch a sugar lump like you

2 They can take in food which has been mixed with water

3 Put a few sugar lumps into a glass of warm water and stir them

4 Soon they will dissolve. You won't be able to see them. But the sugar will still be there

5 Put an onion on top of the glass. Watch it "eat" the sugar mixture, and grow new roots and shoots

The Way Plants Feed

You can watch a plant eating and drinking by giving it water with coloured ink in it

YOU WILL NEED:
a young plant, with roots, stems and leaves
a jar
coloured ink
water
cardboard
scissors

1 Plants take in food from the soil through their roots. It travels up the stems to their flowers and leaves

2 Cut a circle of cardboard, with a hole in the middle, to make a lid. Fit it in the top of a jar

3 Fill the jar with a mixture of water and ink

4 Push the roots of the plant through the hole in the lid into the water

5 Next day you will see the coloured water being sucked up into the plant

Plant Care

Plants need your help and attention as well as food, water and light if they are to flourish. You can watch a plant grow—its roots grow down towards the earth and the shoots grow up towards the sun. Try these experiments

YOU WILL NEED:
3 jars
a handful of dried peas
a sheet of blotting paper
scissors
water
a big cardboard box
sawdust
a cup

1 Put dried peas in a cup of cold water and leave for a day and night

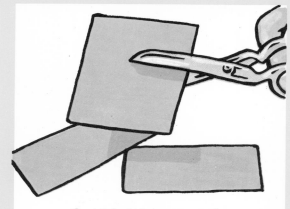

2 Cut blotting paper into three oblong pieces, to fit inside the jars

3 Wrap one piece around the inside of each jar. Fill jars three-quarter full with sawdust

4 Wet the sawdust in one of the jars. Peas have their own supply of food. They don't need any more to start growing

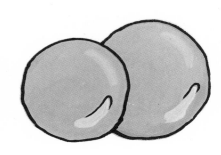

5 Look at a pea. You will see it has a flat tail. This is where the root will grow

6 Push two or three peas down the sides of one jar between the glass and blotting paper

7 Put jar in a light place. Keep the sawdust damp. Soon roots and shoots will start to grow

8 Then leaves and tendrils will grow on the shoots. Your dried peas are young plants

1 Put three more peas into another jar, between the glass and blotting paper. Dampen sawdust and paper

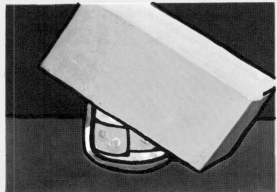

2 Put jar into a dark place and cover with a cardboard box to keep out the light

3 Plant three more peas in the third jar, as before. Put in a light place, but do *not* wet the sawdust and blotting paper

4 After 2 weeks look carefully at all the peas you planted. What has happened to the ones which had no light, or no water?

Growing Plants Outside

Plant a flower outside and watch it grow

YOU WILL NEED:
a trowel
a pansy plant
a watering can
water
plant food
scissors

1 Most plants grow in soil. It holds their roots tightly in place. Try to pull up a weed on a dry day when the soil is hard. It may be quite difficult

2 Big plants like trees have long, thick roots. Little plants like pansies have short, thin roots

3 Plant your pansy in the garden. First make the soil crumbly, like bread-crumbs, using a fork

4 Dig a hole big enough for all the roots. Spread out the roots gently and pat down the soil around them

5 Give your pansy a long drink of water. Make sure that its soil is always damp, but not too wet

6 When the first buds appear, give it some plant food mixed with water. Do this once a week. Pull out any weeds near it

7 Cut off the flower-heads when they die. Your pansy will go on growing new flowers for a long time

Green-Haired Gregory

Grow green hair on Gregory's bald head. You'll have to give him a hair cut every now and then!

YOU WILL NEED:
1 teaspoonful of grass seed
soil
tiny pebbles
a plastic carton
felt-tipped pens
pan-scrubber
scissors
plant food
water

1 Scrub any writing off the carton and dry it well. Draw Gregory's funny face with felt-tipped pens

2 Put a layer of pebbles in the bottom, and fill to the top with damp soil

3 Sprinkle grass seed on to the soil. When it grows it will look like green hair

4 Water Gregory often and feed his hair with plant food once a week

5 When his hair grows too long give Gregory a hair-cut!

Seeds and their Food

When seeds leave their mother plant they have enough food to start growing *roots* and *shoots*

YOU WILL NEED:

a square of ½-inch (1.2cm)
  thick plastic foam
a large baking sheet
grass seed
water

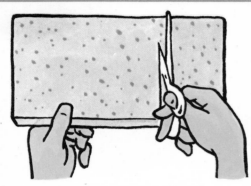

1 Cut a piece of plastic foam so that it is slightly smaller than the baking sheet

2 Put the foam on to the sheet and dampen it. Sprinkle grass seed on top

3 Keep the foam damp, and the grass will grow

4 Lift the square of grass off the sheet and use it as a lawn for your doll's house or petrol station

Bulbs and their Food

Some flowers grow from bulbs. Bulbs are much bigger than seeds. They have enough food to grow *roots* and *shoots* and *leaves* and *flowers*

YOU WILL NEED:

a glass jar
coloured marbles
a hyacinth bulb
a small piece of charcoal
water

1 Fill the jar nearly to the top with marbles. Put the charcoal amongst them

2 Put hyacinth bulb on top of marbles. Pour water into jar until it reaches the bottom of the bulb

3 Put the jar into a cool, dark cupboard. Roots and leaves will soon grow

4 Take the jar out to look at it once a week. Add a little water if the level has dropped

5 When a bud appears at the bottom of the leaves, move into a light place. It will turn into a lovely flower

Fun with Seeds

Seeds are carried away from their mother plant so that they can start to grow somewhere else. You can play games with some seeds. Or you can make them into toys

YOU WILL NEED:
dandelion clocks
sycamore wings
monkey nuts · glue
black and yellow wool
pins · darning needle
rose hips
walnut
cocktail sticks
a sheet of writing paper
plasticine
fir cones, large and small
scissors
paint and paint brush
a circle of cardboard,
    12in (30.5cm) diameter

1 Dandelion seeds are like tiny white parachutes. How many puffs does it take you to blow all the seeds away?

2 Seeds of sycamore and maple trees have wings so they can fly

3 Find a pair of sycamore wings with a small stalk. Push the stalk into a monkey nut and glue

4 Wind stripes of black and yellow wool round the nut

5 Push two pins into one end of the nut, and three pairs of pins underneath. What have you made?

6 Seeds in berries are carried off and dropped by birds. Gather rose hips to make necklace

7 String them together on a piece of wool threaded through a darning needle. Knot the ends together

8 Nuts fall to the ground below their tree. Sometimes they roll away. Make sailing boats from a walnut

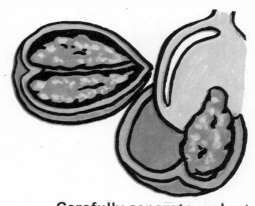

9 Carefully separate walnut into halves and scoop out inside

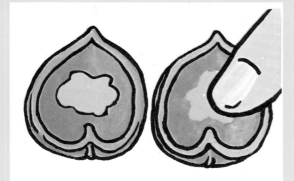

10 Press a tiny piece of plasticine into the bottom of each shell

11 Cut two little squares of paper. Push a stick through each, to make sails. Press sticks into plasticine

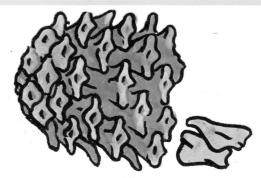

12 Fir cones fall off the tree carrying seeds. Turn a large, opened cone on its side. Cut off some scales from the top

13 Glue a small, unopened cone into the hollow you have made—the pointed end sticking out

14 Paint your duckling

15 Paint cardboard blue. Stick a family of ducks on your duck pond. Put fir cone weeds round the edge of the pond

Who Lives in the Garden?

As well as flowers, vegetables, bushes and trees—insects, birds and animals also live in the garden. Some are our friends—others are enemies

1 A bee might sting you, but he is a friend. He carries pollen from flower to flower and helps them bloom

2 A bee makes honey. Watch him buzzing round the garden. Listen to the noise he makes

3 The ladybird with her red and black spotted coat is a friend. She eats enemy insects which attack roses

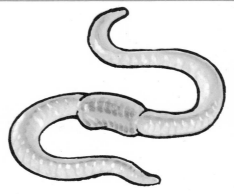

4 Worms are not as pretty as bees or ladybirds. But they are friends

5 They wriggle through the soil and make tunnels. Air travels along the tunnels and helps the plants to grow strong

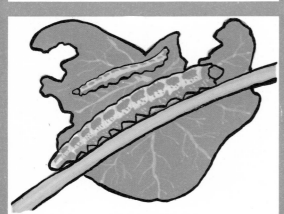

6 Some caterpillars are our enemies. They eat flowers and vegetables

7 But some caterpillars are friends. They only eat weeds

8 Caterpillars are babies. They turn into pretty butterflies when they grow up

9 Red spiders destroy plants. Other spiders do no harm

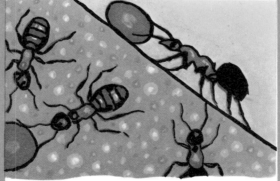

10 Ants are enemies. They carry away seeds and uproot young plants

Slugs and snails are enemies. They eat bulbs, roots and shoots. They kill flowers **11**

12 Often birds live in gardens. They eat enemy insects, but sometimes they eat petals and buds

13 Animals live in some gardens. You might see a mouse, or a hedgehog, a squirrel or rabbit

14 Draw pictures of all the insects, birds and animals you see. Put some in your picture diary, (page 45)

Flowers from Seeds

There are a lot of flowers you can grow this way, but first let's make some pretty painted pots

YOU WILL NEED:
plant pots
paint and paint brushes
stick-on paper shapes

1 Use big and little pots. Grow lots of flowers in big pots, and fewer flowers in little pots

2 Paint the outside of the pots. Paint the top 2 ins (5cm) of the inside

3 When they are dry paint patterns on each one

4 You could paint a funny face

5 Or print your name, or the name of the flower

6 Or you could stick on cut-out paper shapes

7 Here are some flowers you can grow—Alyssum

8 Calendula

9 Candytuft

10 Cornflower

11 Californian Poppy

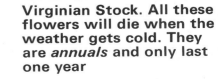

12 Virginian Stock. All these flowers will die when the weather gets cold. They are *annuals* and only last one year

Now Sow your Seeds

You can do this when you see the first green buds on the trees. Remember baby seedlings need special care—don't give them too much water

1 See that there is a hole in the bottom of each pot. Put in a layer of pebbles

2 Use your trowel to fill the pots with damp soil. Make sure it's crumbly. Tiny roots can't grow in lumpy soil

3 Scatter a few seeds on top of the soil. Cover with a thin sprinkling of soil

4 Print the names of the seeds on markers, and put one in each pot. Put outside in a sunny place. Keep the soil damp

5 Keep a piece of paper for each pot. Print numbers from 1 to 100. Write the name of the seeds on top

6 Starting at 1, cross off a number each day, on each page, until the first seedling appears. Circle the corresponding number. Which seeds appeared first?

7 Go on crossing off numbers until the first flowers bloom, then draw a circle. Which seeds flower first?

8 Whenever the seedlings' leaves begin to touch each other, pull out the smallest plants

9 If weeds grow, pull them out and throw them away

10 When the first buds appear feed your plants plant food mixed with water

11 When the flowers bloom, cut some from each pot to make into a bunch

12 Make a hole in the middle of the doily. Pull flower stalks through. Tie ribbon round your pretty posy

13 When the flower-heads in your pots look dead, cut them off. More flowers will bloom

A Tall, Tall Flower

Grow a giant sunflower, (taller than yourself) and give it a funny face. Sunflowers need a deep patch of soil in the sunshine to grow properly

YOU WILL NEED:

sunflower seeds
spade
long measuring stick
marking pen
plant food
scissors
brightly coloured paper
glue
water

1 Dig a wide, deep hole. Put in some plant food. Replace soil and pat down

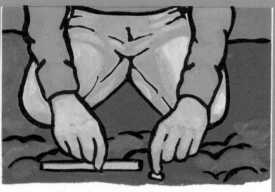

2 Push seeds into soil about 6in (15cm) apart. Cover with soil. Give them a drink of water

3 Put a long stick into the ground next to the seeds. Make a mark on it to show how tall you are

4 When the seedlings appear they will grow quickly. When the leaves of the plants touch each other, pull some out

5 Water plants when the soil gets dry. Feed and measure them each week. Soon they will pass your mark

6 When the leaves have died, cut off the flower-head. Take it indoors to dry. Pull off the petals half-way round

7 Cut out two big circles, two tiny circles and a moon shape from bright paper. Stick them on as eyes, nose and mouth

Flowers from Bulbs

You have grown a hyacinth inside. Now grow some daffodils outside, either in the ground or in a pot

1 When the cold weather begins, dig the soil with your fork. Pull out the weeds

2 With a trowel, make holes 5in deep and 6in apart. (12.5 x 15cm). Put one bulb in each hole. Cover each one with crumbly soil

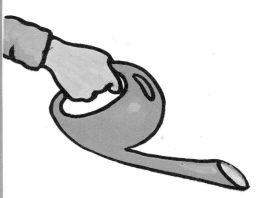

3 Make sure the soil is always damp

4 Green shoots will show through the soil when the weather gets warmer

5 A few weeks later, flowers will start to bloom

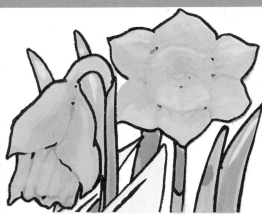

6 When the flowers die, cut off their dead heads

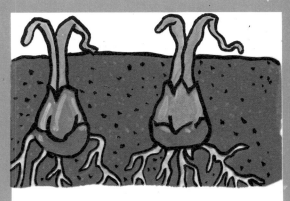

7 When the leaves have withered away, leave the bulbs alone. They will flower again next year

Gardening with no Garden

Even if you have no garden you can grow flowers from seeds, plants or bulbs. Instead of putting them in the ground you can grow them in containers

YOU WILL NEED:
containers
soil
pebbles
trowel
scissors
plastic sheeting
paint and paint brush
bricks
plants and seeds

1 All containers should have holes in the bottom. Prop them up on bricks so water can run away

2 Put a layer of pebbles in the bottom. Fill with soil and then plant seeds, plants or bulbs

3 Water them often. Feed them when buds begin to show. Cut off the flowers' dead heads

4 Paint a bucket. Put in four lobelia plants round the edge and two or three Virginian Stock seedlings in the centre

5 Find a wooden box. Cut plastic sheeting to fit inside. Plant cornflowers

6 An old kitchen sink will look gay planted with golden calendula

7 A barrel makes a good container. Ask a grown-up to cut some holes round the sides 2½in (6.5cm) in diameter

8 Pop two nasturtium seeds into each hole, and six in the top. You can eat nasturtium leaves in salads

9 An old, painted wheelbarrow makes a pretty container. Put plants of trailing lobelia round edges and white alyssum in middle

10 Window-boxes can be fastened to the wall or stand on the window-sill, or ground

11 Lobelia or nasturtiums look good at the front. Grow candytuft and californian poppies behind

12 When the cold weather comes you can take out the dead flowers and plant daffodils in your containers

Make a Poppy Dolly

Grow your own poppies and turn them into dollies for you and your friends

YOU WILL NEED:
poppy seeds
big plant pot
felt-tipped pen
scissors
grass
water

1 Sow poppy seeds outside, in a big pot or in ground

2 Cover with a thin sprinkling of soil. Keep the soil damp. Pull out weeds that grow round the seedlings

3 When the leaves begin to touch each other, pull out the smallest plants

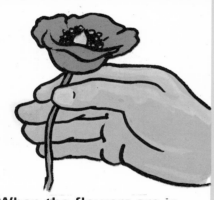

4 When the flowers are in bloom pick one with a long stalk

5 Gently pull its petals down, inside out, so that they look like a skirt round the top of the stalk

6 Pull the hairs off one side of the round head at the top of the stalk to make a face

7 On the poppy's face draw eyes, nose and mouth with a felt-tipped pen

8 Cut off bottom half of stalk. Push it through the top of the petals to make arms

9 Cut a stalk from another poppy. Push inside skirt to make another leg. Cut legs the same length

10 Tie a blade of grass around the middle of the petals as a belt

11 Make a family of poppy dollies like this one

Let's Grow Vegetables

You have grown flowers to look at. Now grow vegetables to eat

1 Choose a patch of soil 2 x 4ft (61 x 122cm) in a light, sunny place, out of the wind

2 Vegetables need more food than flowers. Dig some plant food into the soil

3 Sow seeds and smooth the soil over the top

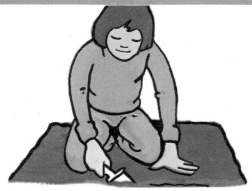

4 With the point of your trowel make a long trench in the soil, ½in deep, and ½in wide. (1.2 x 1.2cm)

5 At one end of trench sprinkle a few lettuce seeds

6 Sprinkle more seeds a measuring stick's distance away. Continue to the end of the trench

7 Put a sprinkle of radish seeds half-way between lettuce seeds

8 Cover seeds with a thin blanket of soil, pat down firmly, and water them

9 Water your vegetable plants whenever the weather is dry

10 Before the plants are 1 inch (2.5cm) tall, pull out smallest ones until there is one left in each sprinkle

11 Pull out any weeds that grow around them

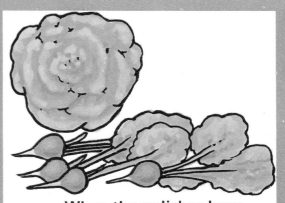

12 When the radishes have round red roots, and the lettuces have large, crisp leaves, they are ready to eat

Vegetables that Climb

Watch peas growing up sticks, and make a bean wigwam

YOU WILL NEED:
pea seeds
runner bean seeds
twiggy sticks
black thread
scissors
3 8-feet (2.4m) canes
a 3 inch (7.5cm)
    measuring stick
garden twine
spade
water

1 With a spade, make a long trench in the soil, 3in deep and 3in wide (7.5 x 7.5cm). Put two pea seeds opposite each other at one end

2 Plant one pea in the middle of the trench a measuring stick's distance away

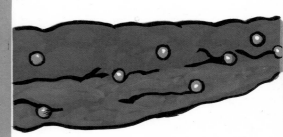

3 Go on planting two peas, then one pea, until the trench is filled. Cover with soil, pat down, and water

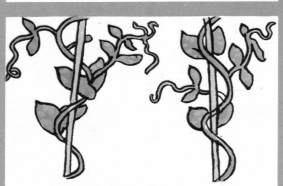

4 When the plants are 3ins (7.5cm) tall push twiggy sticks into the soil beside them. Watch the plants climb up them

5 First the plants will make black and white flowers. These will turn into pods

6 Wind black thread around the sticks to stop birds eating the peas

7 Pick the pods when they look fat and rounded. Take out the peas. Eat them raw or cooked

BEAN WIGWAM

1 Dig a deep big circle and put in a lot of plant food. This is needed to feed the long roots that will grow

2 Push three canes into the soil, 4ft (1.2mm) apart, and tilt them so that their top ends touch

3 Fasten their tops tightly together with garden twine

4 At the bottom of each cane make two holes about 2in (5cm) deep. Put a bean seed into each one

5 Cover the seeds with soil, pat down firmly, and water

6 If two plants grow at the bottom of each cane, pull out the smallest one

7 The beans will grow up the canes and make them into a wigwam covered with red flowers

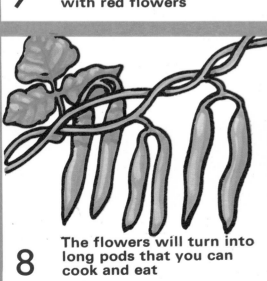

8 The flowers will turn into long pods that you can cook and eat

A Garden on your Window-sill

Start with mustard and cress, and a carrot-top fern

1 Cut two pieces of cloth to fit inside dishes. Place in dishes and dampen

2 Sprinkle one dish with mustard seeds and the other with cress seeds

3 Put both dishes on your window sill. Water them when the cloth begins to get dry

4 When the seedlings are 2-3in (5-7.5cm) tall, cut them and eat them in sandwiches

5 Your mustard will be ready to eat in a week. Your cress will be ready in about two weeks.

6 Get a carrot and pull dead leaves off the top

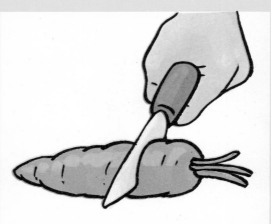

7 Ask Mummy to cut 2in (5cm) off the top end

8 Stand carrot top in a dish

9 Put pebbles round it to hold it in place

10 Pour water into the dish to cover half of the orange part of the carrot

11 Water the carrot often. Don't let it get thirsty

12 Soon new leaves will grow from the carrot-top

13 Your carrot-top plant will go on growing and looking pretty for a long time

Trees from Pips

When you eat grapefruit, oranges or lemons, and apples or pears, you will find tiny pips inside. These are their seeds. Plant them to grow baby trees

YOU WILL NEED:
pips
a cup
a jar
jam pot cover
peat, soil or compost
plant pots
water

1 Put pips into a cup of water for two days

2 Half fill a jar with damp soil. Push pips into it

3 Cover jar, and put in a warm, dark place

4 After about two weeks you will see little shoots

5 Move the jar into the light and take off cover

6 When there are three leaves on each shoot, plant seedlings in a separate pot

7 Give your little trees a few drops of water each day, and watch them grow

A Dwarf Tree

Use one of your own little trees, or a tree seedling you find outside

YOU WILL NEED:
a tree seedling
a gourd or coconut
clear varnish
paintbrush
darning needle
soil of compost
water

1 Cut the top off a gourd or coconut, and scoop out the inside to leave a hollow shell

2 Varnish the outside, and leave to dry. Make holes in the shell, from the inside

3 Fill with soil, and plant your seedling Give it a few drops of water when soil feels dry

4 Cut back straggly branches, and cut off roots as they push through holes

5 If you like, you can grow a dwarf tree in a plastic carton container

Make your own Flower Stall

and fill it with the flowers you have grown

YOU WILL NEED:

Shoe box and lid
Very thick card
2 pieces straight stick
   11in (27.5cm)
2 pieces straight stick
   6in (15cm)
2 corks
round cheese box and lid
PVA paint
household adhesive
kitchen foil
paint brush
ruler
pencil
sharp scissors

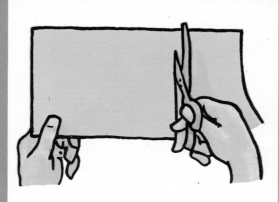

1 Cut thick card 12in (30cm) high and the same length as long side of box

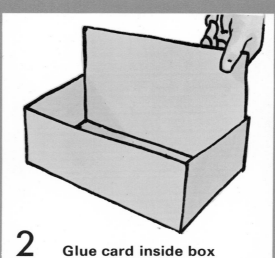

2 Glue card inside box

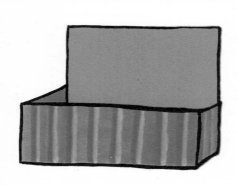

3 Paint box and card inside and outside and leave to dry

4 Paint box lid to make the canopy

5 Paint the cheese box and lid to make wheels

6 Paint corks and sticks in bright colours

7 Glue corks under each corner at one end of box

8 Glue wheels to other end of box

9 Glue the longer sticks to the inside of the front corners

10 Glue the shorter sticks to the front and back of stall to make handles

11 Line bottom of stall with foil

12 Balance lid over top of stall to make canopy

Flower Containers

Look around when you go for a walk, or help in the kitchen. You will be able to arrange flowers, or plant bulbs or seeds, in the things you find

YOU WILL NEED:
plastic bottles and cartons
tins and jars
grapefruit, orange and
    coconut shells
felt-tipped pens
paint and paint brush
stick-on paper shapes
rice, coffee beans, dried
    peas, pebbles, pasta,
    seeds, nuts, shells
tin-foil
string, garden-twine, raffia
scissors · glue

1 Tiny bulbs, like snowdrops or crocuses, look pretty growing in an old teapot

2 or a big cup and saucer

3 or a saucepan

4 Colour plastic cartons with felt-tipped pens, or decorate with cut-out shapes

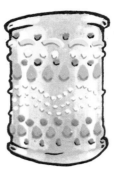

5 Glue grains of rice, coffee beans, pasta shapes tiny pebbles, nuts, seeds or shells to a jar or tin

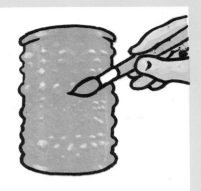

6 Paint them gold, silver, or bright colours and see how pretty they look

7 Paint a tin and let it dry. Make patterns by sticking coloured buttons to the outside

8 Spread glue on the outside of a tin or jar. Wind string, raffia or garden twine around

9 Cut the top end off a plastic bottle. Decorate the bottom end to make a pretty vase

10 You can grow a bulb or seedling in an empty egg-shell or an unusual egg-cup

11 Cut off the top of an orange or grapefruit. Scoop out the inside. Line it with tin-foil

12 Fill it with water or soil. It will last for a few weeks before it withers

13 In the country, or by the sea, you might find a hollow branch or a big shell. Always keep your eyes open

A Garden in a Seed Tray

Miniature gardens are fun to make. When it's all planted you can add a pretty house

YOU WILL NEED:
a seed-tray or shallow box
soil or compost
pencil · cardboard
pebbles or broken crockery
shells or gravel chips
scissors
paints or crayons
water · trowel
grass seed
leptosiphon seed
round mirror
doll's house furniture
tree seedling

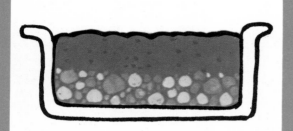

1 In the bottom of a seed tray put a layer of small pebbles or broken crockery. Fill up with fine, damp soil and pat down firmly

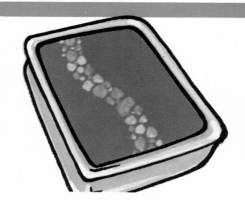

2 Make a path from one short side of tray to the other with gravel chips, or little pebbles

3 With a trowel mark a border 2in (5cm) around edges

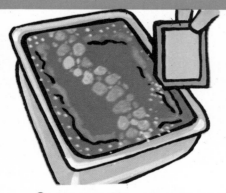

4 Scatter a few sprinkles of leptosiphon seed over the border. Cover with a thin layer of soil

5 Between the border and path on one side of the tray plant a tree seedling

6 Between the border and path on the other side, place a round mirror, as a pond

7 On all the spaces left sprinkle grass seed, and cover with a thin layer of soil

8 Cut out a piece of cardboard as wide as the seed tray but not as long

9 Stand this up behind the tray and make marks to show the top of the tray and the end of the path

10 Draw and colour a house on the cardboard so that the door is at the end of the path

11 Glue the bottom edge of your house to the outside end of the seed-tray

12 Put a doll's house table and chairs on one of the lawns. Keep your garden watered, and the grass cut

Pictures and Pot Pourri

You can make attractive pictures from flowers or make some perfume as a present

YOU WILL NEED:
tin lid or tray
damp soil
flowers
newspapers
salt
cloves
decorated, lidded jars
2 ozs. powdered orris root

PICTURES

1 Fill the lid with damp soil. Press down firmly and draw a pattern in it with your finger

2 Pick small flower-heads off their stalks, and press them into the soil close together

3 Keep your flower picture cool and damp and it will last for a few days

POT POURRI

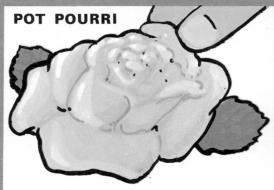

1 Gather sweet-smelling petals, especially rose-petals, when the flowers are dry

2 Spread them on paper and put in a warm, dry place, away from the sun, till the petals are crisp

3 Put a layer in a jar. Sprinkle with salt and a few cloves. Add more petals, salt and cloves till the jar is almost full

4 Add 2 ozs. of powdered orris root which you can buy from a chemist

5 Keep the jar covered for three weeks, and shake it often. Then just take off the lid to smell the pot pourri

Your own Picture Diary

with pictures of all the things you have done

1 Draw twelve boxes on your big sheet of paper, each measuring 6 x 6 ins (15.2 x 15.2cm)

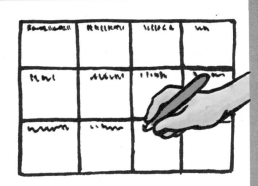

2 Print the name of a month in each box, starting with January

3 Every month, on a paper square, draw a picture of something you have made, or grown, or seen

4 Fasten the square onto the right box on the big sheet of paper with a little piece of sticky tape